Aberdeenshire Library and Information Service
www.aberdeenshire.gov.uk/libraries
Renewals Hotline 01224 661511

2 1 DEC 2012

2 5 MAY 2015

1 1 AUG 2015

ABERDEENSHIRE
LIBRARIES

WITHDRAWN
FROM LIBRARY

1 1 APR 2016

- 4 JAN 2017

2 2 APR 2019

2 6 MAY 2021

1 6 JUN 2022

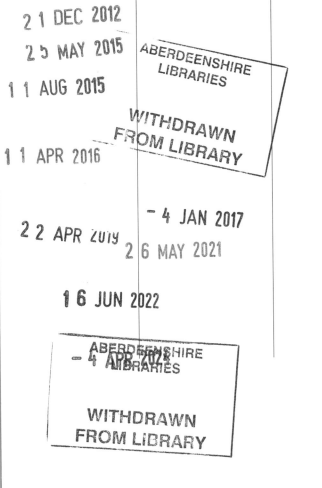

ABERDEENSHIRE
LIBRARIES

- 4 APR 2023

WITHDRAWN
FROM LIBRARY

ABERDEENSHIRE LIBRARIES

1905355

Amazing Planet Earth

THE WORLD'S OCEANS

JEN GREEN

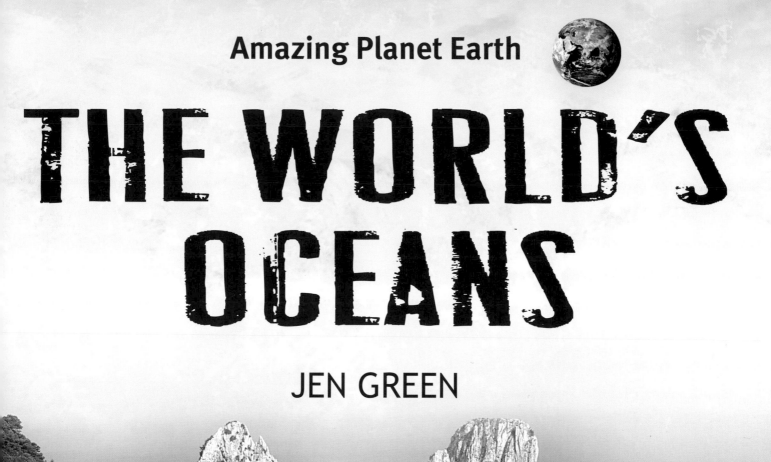

FRANKLIN WATTS
LONDON • SYDNEY

An Appleseed Editions book

First published in 2009 by Franklin Watts

Franklin Watts
338 Euston Road, London NW1 3BH

Franklin Watts Australia
Level 17/207 Kent St, Sydney, NSW 2000

© 2009 Appleseed Editions

Appleseed Editions Ltd
Well House, Friars Hill, Guestling, East Sussex TN35 4ET

Created by Q2AMedia
Editor: Michael Downey
Art Director: Rahul Dhiman
Designers: Harleen Mehta, Ritu Chopra
Picture Researcher: Shreya Sharma
Line Artist: Sibi N. Devasia
Colouring Artists: Aadil Ahmad, Ajay Luthra, Mahender Kumar

J551.
46

All rights reserved. No part of this publication may be reproduced, stored in a
retrieval system or transmitted in any form or by any means, electronic, mechanical,
photocopying, recording or otherwise, without prior permission of the publisher.

ISBN 978 0 7496 8805 9

Dewey classification: 551.46

All words in **bold** can be found in Glossary on pages 30–31.

Website information is correct at time of going to press. However, the publishers cannot
accept liability for any information or links found on third-party websites.

A CIP catalogue for this book is available from the British Library.

Picture credits
t=top b=bottom c=centre l=left r=right
Cover Image: Mana Photo/ Shutterstock.
Back Cover Image: Walt Stepanski/ BigStockPhoto

Insides: Phooey/ iStockphoto: Title Page, Neil Farrin/ Jai/ Corbis: 4, Mollypix/ Shutterstock: 4–5, NASA: 6, Nik Taylor/
Alamy: 7, Phooey/ iStockphoto: 9, Index Stock Imagery/ Photolibrary: 10, Jill Lang/ Shutterstock: 10–11, Arctic-Images/
Flirt Collection/ Photolibrary: 14, Ragnar Th. Sigurdsson/ Photographers Direct: 15, Lloyd S Clements/ Shutterstock: 16–17,
Preckas/ Dreamstime: 17, Bullit Marquez/ Associated Press: 19, Benjamin Lowy/ Corbis: 20, NOAA: 21, NASA: 22,
Ray Fairall/ Associated Press: 23, NOAA: 25, Tomassino/ iStockphoto: 26, FelixStrummer/ iStockphoto: 27,
Benelux/ zefa/ Corbis: 28, Bettmann/ Corbis: 29, Lloyd S Clements/ Shutterstock: 31.
Q2AMedia Art Bank: 6, 8, 12, 13, 18, 24.

Printed in China

Franklin Watts is a division of Hachette Children's Books,
an Hachette UK company.
www.hachette.co.uk

Contents

Five oceans

More than two-thirds of the Earth's surface is covered by salty seas and oceans. Less than one-third is made up of dry land. The world's vast, deep oceans still contain many secrets waiting to be discovered.

Deep blue world

The Earth appears blue when seen from space because so much of it is covered by water in five great oceans. This water reflects blue light shining down from the sky above. The Earth's five oceans are the Pacific Ocean, Atlantic Ocean, Indian Ocean, Arctic Ocean and the stormy Southern Ocean that surrounds Antarctica in the southern hemisphere.

• The Pacific Ocean is dotted with 25,000 islands. Many of these islands are the peaks of mountains that rise from the ocean bed.

• Ocean water is made salty by the minerals that are carried into the oceans by rivers.

DATA FILE

- - - - - - - - - - - -

- A 'sea' is an area of water partly or totally enclosed by land. An 'ocean' is a much larger expanse of water without boundaries.

- The Pacific is the world's largest ocean. It covers nearly 170 million sq. km, or about a third of the Earth's surface. With an average depth of 4,200 metres, it is the world's deepest ocean.

- The world's smallest and shallowest ocean is the Arctic Ocean. Covering an area of 14 million sq. km, its surface is mostly frozen.

Moving in circles

Waves move ocean water around all the time. Most ocean waves are started by winds that sweep across the water's surface. As waves roll across the ocean, the water spins around in a circle. That is why seabirds bob up and down in the same place rather than being swept across the surface. In shallow waters, the seabed blocks this circling motion. This creates white crests as waves break on the water's surface.

Rising and sinking

Surface **currents** are also caused by winds. These currents flow in giant circles called **gyres**. Alongside these, there are other, deeper ocean currents that flow in the opposite direction, as well as places where water rises and sinks.

Currents and tides

Currents are giant underwater rivers that move through the world's vast oceans. These currents can be warm or cold, and have a powerful effect on temperatures on Earth.

Feature: Gulf Stream/North Atlantic Current
Location: North Atlantic Ocean
Width: 85–150 km
Depth: 800–1,200 metres

Giant warming current

Starting in the Gulf of Mexico, the famous ocean current known as the Gulf Stream flows north through the Atlantic Ocean, warming the east coast of North America. The Gulf Stream is called the North Atlantic Current as it continues north-east towards Europe. In winter, the Gulf Stream is up to 13 °C warmer than the waters around it.

• The warm Gulf Stream flows through the Atlantic Ocean along the coast of North America towards Europe.

World's highest tides

The North Atlantic Current warms the shores of western Britain, including the Severn Estuary. This estuary marks the point where Britain's longest river, the River Severn, drains into the Bristol Channel and then out into the Atlantic Ocean. The coastline of the Severn Estuary is washed by some of the world's highest tides. Here, the water rises and falls by up to 15 metres.

Effect of the Moon

Tides are changes in sea level brought about by the Moon. The Moon's **gravity** pulls the ocean towards it, causing a huge mass of water to collect in one place in the ocean. As the Earth spins around, the mass of water moves across the oceans, forming a high tide where it sloshes against coasts. The difference between low and high tide is called the tidal range.

DATA FILE

- The Bay of Fundy in eastern Canada has the biggest tidal range on Earth. Here, the difference between high and low tide can be up to 17 metres.

- The Sun's gravity also affects the world's tides. At a certain time each month, the Sun and Moon line up so that their pulls combine. This produces a very high tide.

• At low tide, the sea drains out of England's Severn Estuary, leaving boats stranded on the mud.

Shaping the seashore

Coasts are the places where the land meets the sea. Altogether, there are over 500,000 kilometres of coasts around the edges of the world's continents and islands.

Collapsing cliffs

On every coast around the world, night and day, waves lap or smash against the shoreline. When powerful waves hit the shore at high tide, they can hurl rocks and pebbles against coastal cliffs. This slowly wears away the cliff in a process called **erosion**. In time, waves can badly damage the bottom of a cliff, causing huge chunks of the cliff to collapse into the sea.

• Ocean waves carve seashore features such as caves, arches and stacks.

Stack

Headland

Arch

Cave

Craggy headlands

On coasts, soft rocks such as chalk wear away more quickly than hard rocks such as **granite**. Areas of soft rock can erode to form wide **bays**, while hard rocks are shaped into craggy headlands. But pounding waves can gradually carve caves in even the toughest of rocks. If two caves are on either side of a headland, they can wear right through to form an arch. When the arch collapses, it leaves a pillar in the sea called a **stack**.

News Flash

Cliff collapse, June 1993

A huge landslide on Britain's east coast has sent a hotel tumbling into the sea. Scarborough's Holbeck Hall Hotel was built in the 1880s. On 3 June it began to slide towards the sea after rain weakened the cliff edge. On 7 June, the cliff gave way completely, and the whole building crashed on to the beach.

Beaches and spits

Along some stretches of coast, the ocean creates new land. This happens because ocean currents carry with them rocky **fragments** and fine sand. When the current slows in sheltered places, such as bays, waves drop the sand and stones to make a beach. Sometimes, a long finger of land forms, stretching out to sea. This is called a **spit**.

- The Twelve Apostles are sea stacks off the Australian coast.

9

Sand islands

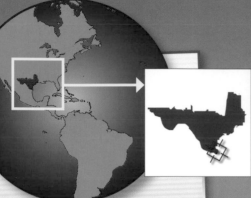

Feature: Padre Island
Location: Southern USA
Length: About 200 km
Speciality: The longest barrier island in the world

• Padre Island, seen here from above, is famous for its sandy beaches.

Over thousands of years, sandy deposits can build up offshore to form long, thin islands. This formation of sand islands has happened along long stretches of coast in the USA.

Slowly moving island

Islands made from sand dropped by the sea are called **barrier islands**. These islands protect the **mainland** from stormy seas. The world's longest barrier island is the USA's Padre Island in the Gulf of Mexico off the southern coast of Texas. Padre Island began forming 4,500 years ago and is now 200 kilometres long. The constant action of the sea is very slowly moving it towards the mainland.

Galveston totally destroyed

Coastal landscapes never stay the same. Change happens fastest during storms, when huge waves lash and pound the shoreline. Sometimes, whole islands can shift sideways, or even be swept away altogether. During a storm in 1900, huge waves swept over the town of Galveston in southern USA. Built on a barrier island, the whole of Galveston was destroyed.

Saved from collapsing

Coastal buildings may need to be rescued when their sandy foundations are attacked by the sea. One such building is the Cape Hatteras Lighthouse, which was in danger of collapsing. Built in the 1870s on a sandy barrier island in south-eastern USA, the lighthouse was moved 1 kilometre inland to a safer place in 1999.

• Cape Hatteras lighthouse now stands on safer ground having been rescued from the sea's pounding waves.

DATA FILE

- The Atlantic coast of North America has one of the world's longest chain of barrier islands. Some 300 islands stretch from the US state of Maine in the north to Mexico in the south.

- In 1992, a **hurricane** shifted an entire barrier island, named Isles Dernieres, in south-eastern USA towards the shore.

Ocean bed

The world's ocean floors have a dramatic, hidden scenery. Beyond the shallow areas of water called continental shelves, which are about 80 kilometres wide, the ocean floor drops steeply to its inky-black depths.

Huge ocean trenches

The beds of the Earth's great oceans are covered by giant **plains** that stretch hundreds of kilometres. In places, these flat areas are broken by sheer cliffs and huge trenches, some of which are deep enough to swallow the world's highest mountains. Long chains of undersea mountains and single peaks are also found on the oceans beds. Some of these mountains are active volcanoes that shoot out red-hot **lava**.

• The craggy scenery on the ocean bed.

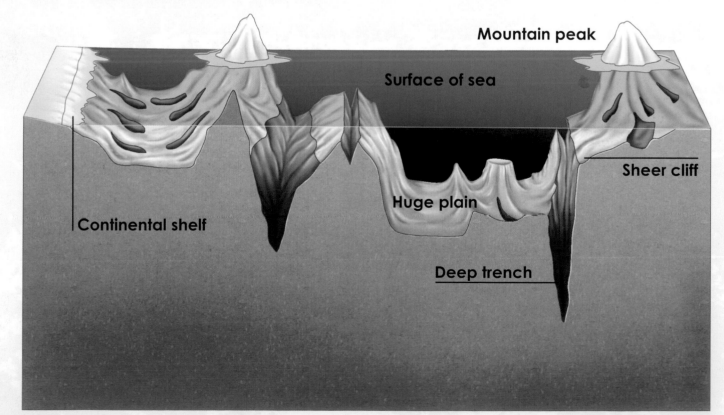

Mountain peak

Surface of sea

Sheer cliff

Huge plain

Continental shelf

Deep trench

Crashing plates

Mountains, volcanoes and trenches are formed by the movement of the huge sections of rock that make up the Earth's **crust**, or outer layer. These rocky sections, called tectonic plates, float on hot, liquid rock below the crust and drift very slowly. These plates can crash into each other or move apart.

Masses of lava

When one plate is pushed below another plate on the ocean bed, a deep trench is formed. Where two plates pull apart, hot lava rises up to fill the gap and what is known as a rift valley is formed. Over time, huge quantities of lava can build up to create a high mountain ridge.

News Flash

Black smokers, December 1977

Scientists exploring the Pacific Ocean in a **submersible** have made a startling discovery. Deep underwater, they have found tall chimneys spouting black clouds of hot, mineral-rich water. Scientists believe these so-called black smokers form on volcanic ridges where tectonic plates are moving apart.

• The Earth's massive tectonic plates fit together like an enormous jigsaw puzzle.

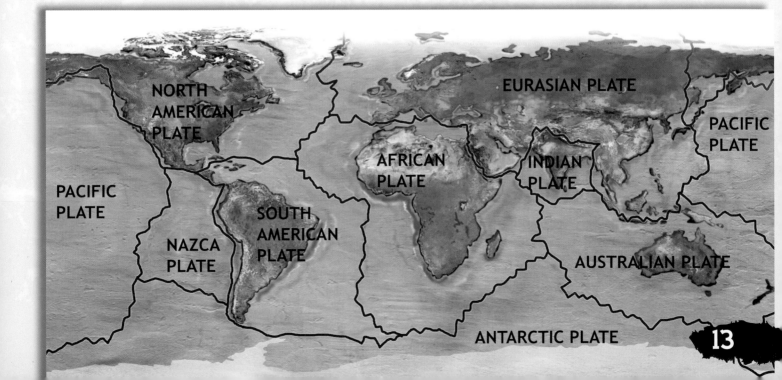

NORTH AMERICAN PLATE

EURASIAN PLATE

PACIFIC PLATE

AFRICAN PLATE

INDIAN PLATE

PACIFIC PLATE

SOUTH AMERICAN PLATE

NAZCA PLATE

AUSTRALIAN PLATE

ANTARCTIC PLATE

Volcanic ridge

A long chain of undersea mountains called the Mid-Atlantic Ridge runs north-to-south down the centre of the Atlantic Ocean. This ridge stretches from Iceland down to the Southern Ocean.

Ever-widening ocean

The Atlantic Ocean has been forming over millions of years. It is still getting wider today by about 2 centimetres a year. Originally, there was no ocean. The huge hollow for the ocean, which filled with water, gradually formed as some of the Earth's continents were pushed apart by volcanic activity. These volcanoes also formed the mountains of the Mid-Atlantic Ridge.

• Undersea volcanoes spill out red-hot lava along parts of the Mid-Atlantic Ridge.

Feature: Mid-Atlantic Ridge
Location: Runs the length of the Atlantic Ocean
Length: 11,300 km

Creation of Iceland

Many of the massive mountains that make up the Mid-Atlantic Ridge rise 4,000 metres above the sea floor. In most places, the tops of these mountains are about 2,500 metres below the surface of the Atlantic Ocean. But in other regions, so much lava has built up that an island has formed. Iceland is an island that has formed in this way. Iceland is made up of a dark rock called basalt that forms when red-hot lava spills out of a volcano and is cooled quickly by sea water. Today, there is still plenty of volcanic activity on Iceland and in the nearby ocean bed.

- In 1963, the volcanic island of Surtsey was formed in the North Atlantic.

News Flash

Birth of Surtsey, November 1963

A new island has appeared in the icy North Atlantic. On 15 November 1963, fishermen watched as a pillar of black smoke rose from the ocean. Lava soon broke the surface to form an island, which has been named Surtsey after the Icelandic god of fire.

Dangerous waters

The world's oceans hold many perils, both for ships and for people living on the coast. Powerful waves and hidden rocks can smash and sink ships, while violent storms can rip through coastal towns.

Terrifying waters

Most sailors have experienced the truly terrifying power of the sea. Sudden and violent storms can cause extremely rough seas. Lashing winds are whipped up, and surging, crashing waves smash on to ships and batter exposed coasts. These conditions are especially deadly for small sailing vessels. When caught in the middle of a storm, these boats are helpless against the raging sea.

- The bright beams of lighthouses warn ships away from jagged rocks at night.

Jagged rocks

Scientists think that there could be as many as three million ships lying at the bottom of the world's seas and oceans. Most of them were sunk by the jagged rocks and sandbanks that lie hidden under the water's surface, waiting to rip open or trap a ship. When a ship's captain has to navigate through fog out at sea, things can get even more dangerous. Sometimes, ships collide when sailing through thick fog.

News Flash

Pacific Ocean, 6 February 1933

The US ship *Ramapo* has been caught in a violent storm in the Pacific as it sailed home to the United States from the Philippines. The crew reported waves towering up to 34 metres high, the highest ever recorded.

Underwater hazards

What can be done to help guard against these dangers? Lighthouses and buoys play an important part in warning ships of nearby reefs and other perils. Ships are now also equipped with **sonar** devices that detect underwater hazards. Modern **navigation** equipment and accurate weather reports help ships to steer a safe course through even the most dangerous conditions.

• Huge numbers of ships have sunk in the oceans over the centuries.

Deadly tsunamis

Undersea volcanic explosions and earthquakes can cause giant waves called tsunamis. These killer waves can travel across oceans for thousands of kilometres.

Waves sweeping ashore

On 26 December 2004, a powerful earthquake struck off the coast of Indonesia. This caused tsunamis to shoot out in all directions from the earthquake's centre, called its 'epicentre'. Giant waves hit the Aceh region of northern Sumatra just 15 minutes later, and reached Thailand and Malaysia in 90 minutes. Here, tourists witnessed a terrifying sight. First the sea drained away from beaches, then huge waves rolled in and swept ashore.

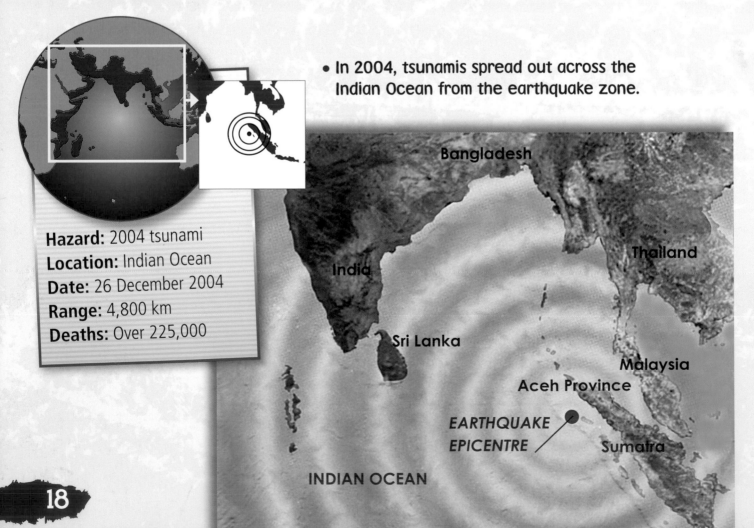

• In 2004, tsunamis spread out across the Indian Ocean from the earthquake zone.

Hazard: 2004 tsunami
Location: Indian Ocean
Date: 26 December 2004
Range: 4,800 km
Deaths: Over 225,000

Bangladesh

Thailand

India

Sri Lanka

Malaysia

Aceh Province

EARTHQUAKE
EPICENTRE

Sumatra

INDIAN OCEAN

• Over 130,000 people died in the city of Banda Aceh in Sumatra after the earthquake and tsunami.

Water rearing up

In the open ocean, tsunamis are low waves about a metre high. They travel at hundreds of kilometres per hour. It is only when they reach shore that they slow down and rear up much higher. In 2004, it took two hours after the earthquake struck for tsunami waves to reach Sri Lanka and southern India. Here, people, animals and even vehicles were swept along by the swirling water. Seven hours after the earthquake, the tsunamis had reached Africa, 4,800 kilometres away.

News Flash

26 December 2004

Coasts around the Indian Ocean have been hit by tsunamis following a major earthquake on the seabed. Over 200,000 people are feared dead. The Indonesian city of Banda Aceh has suffered the worst damage. Experts are calling this the worst natural disaster of the early 21st century.

Millions made homeless

The day after the Indian Ocean tsunamis, the terrible damage that the disaster had caused became clear for the whole world to see. Towns and villages all around the Indian Ocean were destroyed and millions of people had lost their homes. As well as devastating Sumatra, the tragedy brought death and destruction to Thailand. Here, many fishing boats were wrecked and **crops** were ruined. In Sri Lanka, to the west, about 1,500 people died. Even further west, in Somalia in Africa, more than 300 people were killed.

• After the 2004 tsunami disaster, relief workers had to use elephants to move debris.

Looking for survivors

Countries around the world sent food, medicines, tents for shelter and rescue workers to the disaster region. The first task was to search ruined buildings for any survivors. After this, the work of clearing the debris began so that people could start to rebuild their shattered lives.

Sounding the alarm

A tsunami warning system is now being set up in the Indian Ocean. A similar system already exists in the Pacific Ocean. Sensors on the sea bed warn of earthquakes and volcanic **eruptions** that can trigger tsunamis. If the alarm is given, people know to run as quickly as possible to higher ground, where they will be safe.

• This buoy marks the site of an earthquake sensor on the sea bed. It is part of a tsunami warning system.

DATA FILE

- The word tsunami means 'harbour wave' in Japanese.

- Tsunamis are hardly noticeable out at sea. They rear up as they reach harbours and coasts.

- In 1896, the Japanese island of Honshu was wrecked by tsunamis, and 28,000 people died. Fishermen working out to sea barely noticed the waves as they passed under their fishing boats.

- In 1964, an earthquake in Alaska set off tsunamis that swelled to a height of 12 metres. These are still among the highest ever recorded.

Storm surges

High seas called storm surges can be whipped up by storms and hurricanes. In 1992, a violent hurricane named Andrew produced a storm surge that badly battered Florida, in south-eastern USA.

Heavy floods

Hurricanes are very powerful storms that develop over warm seas in summer. Winds start to spin around a column of calm air in the centre, called the eye. These winds, which whirl around at up to 320 km/h, suck up water from the ocean. A mound of water piles up below the eye – this is the **storm surge**. When the hurricane hits land, the storm surge acts like a very high tide, often causing floods and massive destruction.

• An aerial photograph of Hurricane Andrew whirling close to Florida in the USA.

Trail of destruction

In August 1992, Hurricane Andrew blew in from the ocean, bringing with it a storm surge 5 metres high. Swirling water and high winds picked up trucks, boats and even aircraft and tossed them further inland. The hurricane raged across the tip of Florida, leaving a trail of destruction about 40 kilometres wide. One of the most destructive storms of the 20th century, Hurricane Andrew caused an amazing $26 billion of damage.

- The violent power of Hurricane Andrew in 1992 devastated many towns in Florida.

DATA FILE

- Hurricanes and storm surges have caused great destruction in low-lying Bangladesh, on the shores of the Indian Ocean. In 1970, a hurricane caused widespread flooding here, and 500,000 people died.

- Hurricanes are known as typhoons in the Pacific. In the Indian Ocean, people call them cyclones.

- In 2005, Hurricane Katrina flooded the city of New Orleans in southern USA. Over 1,800 people died.

Giant icebergs

Ice is a major hazard in waters around the North and South poles. In the north, icebergs drift south from the Arctic to menace ships in the North Atlantic.

Iceberg

Canada
USA

Hazard: Iceberg
Location: North Atlantic
Incident: Sinking of the *Titanic*
Date: 15 April 1912
Deaths: 1,490

Mass of hidden ice

Icebergs are huge chunks of ice that break off glaciers in the Earth's **polar regions**. Less than a fifth of an iceberg shows above the water's surface, the rest lying underwater. That is why it is so dangerous for ships to approach these floating masses of ice.

- The *Titanic* was supposed to be unsinkable, but it dropped to the bottom of the Atlantic Ocean when it hit an iceberg.

Tragedy strikes

The *Titanic* was one of the largest, most luxurious ships ever built. It was just four days into its first voyage from Britain to New York in April 1912 when it struck an iceberg. The **liner** sank in less than three hours, and 1,490 passengers and crew drowned. Only 700 people, mostly women and children, escaped in lifeboats.

Wreck discovered

For 70 years, the *Titanic* lay hidden on the bed of the Atlantic Ocean. In 1985, a diving team found the wreck 4,000 metres below the surface. Shortly after, a small US Navy submersible called *Alvin* was sent down to look over the wreck. Later, many objects were recovered from the ship.

Deep-sea creatures

Alvin is the world's most famous submersible. In 1977, scientists in *Alvin* discovered the first black smokers that form in volcanic ridges in the ocean. *Alvin* has also been used to bring deep-sea creatures to the surface. Just 7 metres long, it carries three people.

- The submersible *Alvin* has made many important discoveries in the ocean depths.

News Flash

15 April 1912

The liner *Titanic* has met with disaster in the North Atlantic. The crew radioed for help shortly after midnight on 15 April after hitting an iceberg, but sank two hours later. Rescue ships arrived in time to pick up survivors in lifeboats, but more than 1,400 souls went down with the ship.

Rising seas

Today, sea levels are rising and the polar ice-caps are getting smaller. In the future, this may lead to severe flooding in coastal areas.

Melting ice

During long, cold periods called **Ice Ages**, ice covered much of the land. Sea levels were lower because so much water was frozen on land. During the last Ice Age, which ended about 10,000 years ago, sea levels were up to 90 metres lower than today. When the **climate** warmed, the ice melted, and the sea rose to flood coastal valleys. This formed steep-sided inlets called **fjords** on some coasts.

• Fjords are steep-sided inlets. These form when the sea floods a coastal valley.

Earth heating up

The world is slowly getting warmer because some gases in the atmosphere are trapping the Sun's heat close to Earth. Scientists call this **global warming**. The gases are produced when we burn **fossil fuels**, such as oil and coal, in our power stations, factories, homes and cars.

Danger of flooding

Ice in the polar regions has started to melt because of this global warming. As the oceans expand and the water levels rise, more and more low-lying islands and coastal cities will be put in danger of flooding.

- **Rising seas could one day flood these low-lying islands in the Indian Ocean.**

DATA FILE

- World temperatures rose by about 0.5 °C in the 20th century. They went up fastest in the polar regions.

- Scientists think that temperatures may rise by 2–4 °C by the year 2100.

- A rise of 4 °C would cause ice to melt in the polar regions, increasing the risk of flooding.

- In the late 1990s, a huge chunk of ice broke off an ice shelf in Antarctica and floated away. Ice frequently breaks off the ice shelf, but this was the biggest chunk so far.

- Sea levels have risen by 15–20 cm in the last 100 years due to melting polar ice caps.

Threatened coast

Hazard: Rising sea levels
Location: The Netherlands
Area: 40,840 sq. km, of
which 7,700 sq. km is
reclaimed land
Flood-prone areas:
Reclaimed land along
the coast

The Netherlands is one of the lowest-lying countries in the world. It has been hit by floods many times in history. Now it is threatened by rising sea levels because of global warming.

Reclaiming land

Dutch people have been reclaiming land from the sea for centuries. High walls called **dykes** have been built on coasts to keep the North Sea from flooding land. Water is pumped out of the marshy ground behind the dykes to create fields called **polders**.

• These pillars, part of the flood defences in the Netherlands, protect the land from the sea.

Repairing the dykes

Low-lying parts of the Netherlands have flooded many times in past centuries. In 1953, a violent storm caused a storm surge in the North Sea. Water broke through the dykes and flooded up to 2,000 sq. km of land. When the sea finally retreated, the damaged dykes took many months to repair. After this, the Dutch people built a network of flood barriers to protect their country from the destructive power of the sea.

- In 1953, flooding caused by a storm surge left many towns in the Netherlands badly damaged. Cold temperatures made the situation worse for many of the victims of the floods.

Safeguarding coasts

So what can be done to protect low-lying countries from the growing danger of flooding caused by global warming? Most scientists believe that the first, and most urgent, step we can take is to use much less oil and coal, which damage the atmosphere. Instead, there should be a great effort around the world to switch to using other types of fuels and energies that produce less pollution.

News Flash

2 February 1953

The Netherlands and eastern England have been hit by floods following a severe storm. Winds of 115 km/h piled sea water into the narrow channel of the North Sea. Over 80 dykes have collapsed in Holland, and 1,800 people are feared dead.

Glossary

barrier island an island made of sand that has been deposited by the sea

bay a curving inlet on the coast

black smoker an undersea volcano that spouts clouds of hot, dark, mineral-rich water

climate the long-term weather pattern of a region

crops plants that are grown each year to feed people and animals

current a regular flow of water in a certain direction

dyke a bank built to prevent flooding by a river or the sea

erosion the wearing away of rocks by water, wind or ice

eruption when a volcano becomes active and gives off ash, gas and lava

fjord a steep-sided inlet formed when the sea floods a deep valley by the coast

fossil fuel a fuel that is formed in the Earth's crust

fragment a small piece

global warming a general rise in temperatures, caused by a build-up of gases in the air which trap the Sun's heat

granite a very tough rock often used in the construction of buildings

gravity the pulling power of the Earth, Moon, Sun or another huge object in space

gyre a huge circular ocean current

hurricane a large, powerful spinning storm. Hurricanes are also called cyclones and typhoons

Ice Age a long, cold period in our planet's history, during which ice covered more of the Earth's land than it does now

lava hot, melted rock from underground that surges up to the surface when a volcano erupts

liner a large and luxurious passenger ship that sails regularly between specific ports

mainland the main area of a country, not including any islands that may also form part of that country

navigation the guiding of ships and aircraft from one place to another

plain a large area of land that is flat

polar regions areas at or around the North and South poles

polder a field made from reclaimed land

sonar a device that uses sound waves to find objects underwater

spit a sandy finger of land stretching out to sea

stack a pillar of rock standing in the sea

storm surge a mound of water whipped up by a storm or hurricane

submersible an underwater craft

Index

Webfinder

www.kidsgeo.com/geography-for-kids/0134-the-earths-oceans.php

http://oceanservice.noaa.gov/education/welcome.html
Facts about the oceans

http://oceanservice.noaa.gov/education/kits/tides/tides01_intro.html
A look at ocean tides and currents

www.fema.gov/hazard/tsunami/index.shtm
Information about what to do if a tsunami threatens

www.sio.ucsd.edu/voyager/earth_puzzle/recycling_plates.html
A look at the basics of plate tectonics

www.climate.noaa.gov/education/hurricanes/hurricane_basics.pdf
Facts about hurricanes